ABOUT PAWS OF HONOR

Paws Of Honor's mission is to provide quality routine and specialized veterinary care for retired military and local, state, and federal law enforcement K9s across the nation, at no charge to their handlers' who become financially responsible for them upon retirement.

DEDICATION

To our loyal best friends and brave partners who selfishly and lovingly walk, for a short time, with us through life...

FOR CHESSIE

I like to think he had a good life because of me, but I know that my life was made so much better by him. Rest easy buddy. It was truly an honor to be your person. I hope Clint is throwing the tennis ball for you.

In recognition and appreciation for supporting
this title and our program Paws Of Honor
wishes to recognize these sponsors.

Leslie L Alexander Foundation

Thank You for your continued
generous contributions to our organization.

The Working Dog Coffee Company provides roasted-to-order premium coffees, apparel, drinkware, and canine products, in support of rescue, rehabilitation, and re-homing of our canine working partners and companions.

https://workingdogcoffeecompany.com/

Paws of Honor

How I Became A
Hero

Written by MH DeLisle
Illustrated by AJ Wanegar

First Published in 2020 in the United States of America
by Treehouse Publishing Group
Jamestown, Tennessee, USA
E: press@treehousetoons.com
W: www.TreehouseToons.com

Credits and benefits to non-profit organization
Paws of Honor
W: www.pawsofhonor.org

Paws of Honor Series
First Title: How I Became A Hero
ISBN#978-107360569-0-5

M H DeLisle as the author
AJ Wanegar as the illustrator

Yes, you heard me right! I'm a hero! But, like every other hero, there was a time when I was- well- little. I was scrappy and full of silly, trouble-making energy - just like you!

I think a lot about my days as a puppy. They were far from boring. I was lucky to have my siblings to play with.

Mama often took us into the back yard, where there were always plenty of toys.

The ball was my favorite.

I played with it every day.

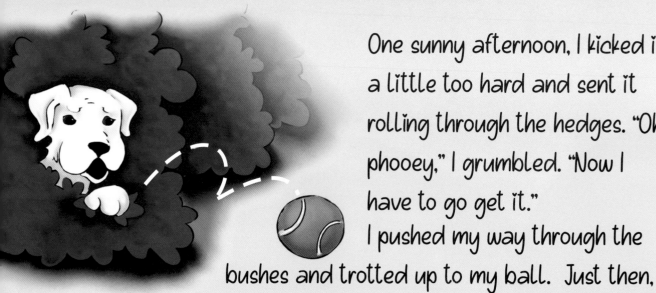

One sunny afternoon, I kicked it a little too hard and sent it rolling through the hedges. "Oh phooey," I grumbled. "Now I have to go get it."

I pushed my way through the bushes and trotted up to my ball. Just then, a lightning-fast puppy came speeding out of the neighbor's house.

She barked and swerved until she stopped right in front of me.
Our eyes met for a second and I couldn't help but stare.
I thought, "WOW! She is magnificent."

But before I could even blink...
she took my ball! I chased her around the yard until I got it
back. By then, we were both exhausted. The whole thing ended
with us laughing and panting as we rolled
in the grass. She even sounded
pretty when she spoke.

Hi, I'm Dutchess!

Over the weeks that followed, we spent
lots of time together. Dutchess and I challenged
each other to races and showed off the tricks we learned.
We'd play all day until the sun went down. That's how we
became best friends.

Back then, we were just
two young friends having
fun. We didn't understand
how much life could change.
So when it did, I was heartbroken:
I had to leave my best friend! I was
sad and confused as I peered out the back window of the truck.
Just by looking at her, I could tell that Dutchess felt the same.
Leaving her side was a very hard thing to do.

"Where was this truck going to bring me?" I had so many questions floating around in my mind, and they made me a nervous wreck. The sound of the truck's rumbling startled me. The sight of houses and trees speeding by was far from comforting.

At the time, I had no idea that
I was on my way to a training
program for service dogs. And in
that place, I'd begin an exciting and inspiring journey.
As I climbed out of the vehicle, the man taking my leash
said, "Hi Chessie, welcome to Puppies Behind Bars."

I was an even bigger
bundle of jittery nerves
when we stepped inside.
There were a lot of people
and dogs that I didn't know in that building.
My senses were filled with strange noises and even stranger
scents. Unfamiliar voices chatted away. The creaking and
clanging of doors opening and closing filled the air.

So many sights and sounds became a little bit overwhelming. It was hard to contain my nervous energy and excitement. I wanted to jump around and bark so badly! Just then, I heard a commanding voice echo throughout the halls. "Sit, Chessie! Sit, boy!" I froze instantly "Ladies and gentlemen, meet my puppy raiser, Clint." He was the most confident human being I had ever met. His voice had risen effortlessly above all the activity around me. I couldn't help but notice him immediately!

Yes, my raiser had found me at just the right moment and turned out to be a great match for me. Clint was patient, friendly, and knew exactly when to use his stern voice. It was that voice that taught me how to stay focused and helped me to reach my goals.

In the beginning, "No, Chessie, no" was a familiar phrase I often heard. But with patience, practice, and Clint to teach me, I found myself learning a lot. I grew up to be polite, noble, and compassionate. I also learned how to make smart decisions quickly in the face of uncertainty.

I stayed at Puppies Behind Bars for a good, long while. I knew that some time had passed because I had grown into a big dog. I trained with Clint for the entire time, learning more and more each day. Thanks to him, I became a really smart pooch!

My one-on-one time with Clint was always fun. But sometimes, I got to play with the other dogs too! We spent many hours chasing each other outside and swimming in a nearby river.

One dog named Ace loved it when we worked together to collect sticks in the water. We'd even carry them back to our humans on the bank. It felt great to be a part of a team! Playing "fetch" with toys, chasing other dogs, and swimming around were actually parts of my training.

14

The tennis balls and squeakers that I played with really came in handy. They were sometimes used as tools to help me overcome my fears. I remember being a little hesitant about getting my fur wet.

That made me not want to go into the river at first. But then, Clint tossed my ball out into the water. "Fetch it, Chessie! Yes, that's it!" he commanded. With lots of courage and a big splash, I went straight in after it.

I really loved learning from Clint. I could tell that he loved teaching me too. I was determined to make him proud. I tried hard to make as few mistakes as possible. Soon our training became routine for me. That helped me to become really good at understanding what Clint expected.

I thought I might like to stay with Clint forever. But life's full of surprises. I discovered that fact when I heard Clint talking to his supervisor.

Chessie has a lot of energy. Are you certain that he wouldn't be better suited for another job?

Clint pointed out.

Well, it's possible that he will calm down as he gets older. He has a lot of potential,

the supervisor said.

I could hear the hesitation in Clint's voice. "All right, we'll give it a try," he said as he sat down in a strange-looking chair with wheels. That rolling chair scared me! I wondered, "Will it run me over?" It rolled forward ever so slightly and I panicked. I began barking and running in circles.

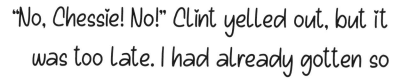

"No, Chessie! No!" Clint yelled out, but it was too late. I had already gotten so carried away that I found myself in his lap. Yeah, Clint was right. I was not ready for that new job at all. The supervisor agreed, "Okay, the Wounded Warriors Project definitely is out of the question."

Ah, the Wounded Warriors Project . . . That was apparently going to be my new job. Well, it was until I mucked up the scary-chair-with-wheels test. I was incredibly discouraged. Working in that program sounded like a great job to have! I would have been helping a veteran live his or her life the very best that they can. Veterans are retired soldiers who defended our nation. I would have been proud to do that job.

Clint took me back to our room, where I sulked in my bed. I mulled over my failed attempt to become a service dog for veterans. I sobbed about how I disappointed Clint. "I'd never become a hero this way!" I thought. Just then, I heard faint voices, prompting me to press my ear against the wall. It was the supervisor and Clint speaking. Their discussion made me feel uneasy.

19

"He failed that test miserably. He needs a job that makes use of all that energy. What about the water rescue program?" asked the supervisor. "The water rescue program?" Clint repeated.

20

"Gosh, I don't know about that. He likes the river well enough, but the ocean might be another matter entirely. I'd need to work with him some more while I think about it."

I thought about it too. The water rescue program teaches dogs to rescue humans who are struggling in the water.

These K9s have to be very brave and strong. They swim in the rough currents of large rivers and oceans. That sounds like a really cool job to me! I mean, who wouldn't want to go swimming every day? I never got to train for that program, but I was just as happy when my training with Clint continued.

He still believed in me. That's a sign of trust and faith! I promised myself that I wouldn't let him down again. I was determined to keep that promise as Clint and I played a new game. He started hiding things for me to find. I got to stick my nose under things and into corners. Clint always found a new spot to tuck a treat or toy into.

Sniffing around and finding stuff was easy for me. It was fun, fast-paced and I loved it. There was one thing that wasn't quite adding up though. Another person was joining us for training. Clint called her Carla. I knew that because I heard Clint speaking with her.

She said,

He's a natural.

Her compliment gave me the feeling that I was going to experience another big change.

Ever since I met Carla, she had been showing up to work with Clint and me. I made sure to train really hard and impress them both. It was very important that I did well in my efforts and that I got to see their nods of approval.

After a short time, my instincts were proven right: things really were going to change again. But this time, that change came with some news - incredible news!

I was - deep breaths, Chessie. . . deep breaths - chosen to be . . . an Explosive Detection K9 Officer!

When that news was out in the open, Clint looked at me with tearful eyes. He said, "Listen, buddy, you're going to be doing a very important job! But I know you can handle it and am very proud of you." I was so happy that my effort had finally paid off! But still, I was worried. Where would I go? Who would I be working with next?

I felt reassured when Carla joined us. She knelt down next to Clint and spoke kindly to me. She said, "Come on, Chessie. . . Let's go become heroes together!" She put a harness with a badge on me and I left Puppies Behind Bars with her by my side.

Outside, an official K9 Officer's squad car was waiting. Carla opened up the door, revealing some nice-looking seats. I leapt excitedly into the back of the posh vehicle. "Wow, it's really quite comfy in here!" I thought to myself.

Carla climbed into the driver's seat and started the car. As we drove away, I thought about everything that Clint and I had accomplished together. Each memory that came to mind filled me with both joy and sorrow. I was proud of myself, but saying goodbye was still hard.

We drove for a while, passing by houses and trees. The squad car came to a steady halt. Carla rolled down the window to speak with a mother and her child. She said, "Hello. How are you today?"

30

I didn't understand why the boy looked a tad scared. Carla smiled warmly as she looked at the child. She asked, "Son, have you ever met a police dog in person?" He replied, "No, Ma'am." The child's expression changed from fear to delight as Carla lowered my window. The boy peeked into the vehicle and I sat up proudly.

"Look Mom, he's so good! He's not even trying to jump out." The boy's eyes widened with surprise. Carla turned the lights and siren on! In response, the child clapped and giggled gleefully. That seemed to make his mother happy too.

Thank you for showing us your beautiful dog, she said with a grin.

I watched the scenery again as we continued down the road.
The houses and trees were soon replaced by a parking lot. I
was on alert when I saw other squad cars lined up in a row.
We came to a stop.

33

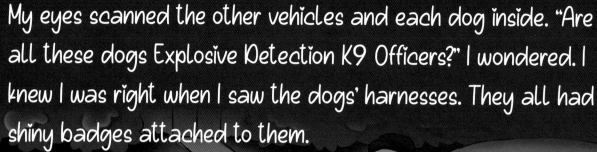

My eyes scanned the other vehicles and each dog inside. "Are all these dogs Explosive Detection K9 Officers?" I wondered. I knew I was right when I saw the dogs' harnesses. They all had shiny badges attached to them.

But that wasn't what caused me to freeze in place. I could've sworn I saw a very familiar face. "It- it couldn't be, could it? Is that. . . Dutchess?"

COMING SOON

To get information on each new title in this series like and follow us on Facebook

wwwfacebook.com/pawsofhonor
www.pawsofhonor.org

In recognition and appreciation for supporting
this title and our program Paws Of Honor
wishes to recognize these sponsors.

An award winning Georgia golf and
lake community bordered by 9 miles
of Lake Oconee shoreline. Enjoy
resort style living in a well
established gated community with
premium amenities and the finest
golf you can play in the Southeast.

https://www.harborclub.com/